Leave The Last Cookie For Someone Else

Thoughts On Navigating Life
With Balance, Influence & Contentment

Richard McKeown

P.O.P

Press On Press

© 2021 Press On Press
All Rights Reserved

These contents may not be reproduced, redistributed or retransmitted in any form, including but not limited to, printed and digital formats without the expressed written consent of the author.

Limited portions may be quoted when attributed to:
"Leave the Last Cookie for Someone Else by Richard McKeown"

Cover photography by Mark McCrary

Cover background uses resources from Freepik.com

Editing and Design by Chandler Business Solutions.

ISBN: 979-8-70-438990-3

*Dedicated to
Evan, Ella, Cash, Edie, Annie and Sophia.

May your lives bring you
the blessings, love and joy
you bring to mine.*

Also by Richard McKeown
State of Redemption

Introduction

    Over the years I have made a habit of jotting down thoughts born of lessons learned through experience, observation and reflection. Or some combination thereof.

    Some lessons have been harder than others; sweeter than others; more defining than others. They have come through the joys and sorrows, wins and losses, good times and bad that attend any life. I am richer for having learned them through a life that's been neither extraordinary, renowned or so far as I know, notorious.

    Along the way, I have entertained the notion that what I have learned might be helpful to my grandchildren someday. It is to them this little book is dedicated.

    And ego, being a powerful thing, has suggested others might find these observations and reflections insightful and valuable as they live and learn along life's way. Thus, Leave the Last Cookie for Someone Else.

    In these pages you will not find much narrative. Very little, in fact. What you will find are concise thoughts intended to encourage you and enrich not only your life, but the lives of those with whom you live, work, play, mentor and love.

Richard McKeown
June 2021

Leave The Last Cookie For Someone Else

Just be nice.

Richard McKeown

Rarely do people get in trouble
for what they don't say.

Leave The Last Cookie For Someone Else

Some things can't be taught.
They can only be learned.

Richard McKeown

Help those who can't help themselves.
And those who can't help you.

Leave The Last Cookie For Someone Else

The best givers are cheerful.
And anonymous.

Richard McKeown

More is learned in a season of adversity than in a lifetime of affluence.

Leave The Last Cookie For Someone Else

Unity and uniformity
are not the same things.

Richard McKeown

The finer the print,
the more carefully it should be read.

Leave The Last Cookie For Someone Else

We are all smart and we are all stupid.
It's just about different things.

Richard McKeown

Wiser are those who ask questions
more than they make statements.

Leave The Last Cookie For Someone Else

There is a big difference between listening and waiting to talk.

Richard McKeown

Freedom of choice does not come with freedom from consequences.

Leave The Last Cookie For Someone Else

Don't expect your children to know now
all you have learned since then.

Richard McKeown

Good manners
and common courtesy
always matter.

Leave The Last Cookie For Someone Else

Sacrifices made cost less
than sacrifices required.

Richard McKeown

Leave the last cookie for someone else.

Leave The Last Cookie For Someone Else

**Be thankful
all you have to complain about
is all you have to complain about.**

Richard McKeown

The unhappy are usually ungrateful.
The ungrateful are usually unhappy.

Leave The Last Cookie For Someone Else

Good communication is not
'You agree with me.'

Richard McKeown

Vote for candidates
who most agree with you,
not vice versa.

Leave The Last Cookie For Someone Else

There's a difference
between knowing how to do things
and knowing what needs to be done.

Richard McKeown

Early influences are lasting ones,
for better or worse.

Leave The Last Cookie For Someone Else

You don't want the least expensive.
You don't need the most expensive.

Richard McKeown

Excessive slumber is exhausting.

Leave The Last Cookie For Someone Else

People keep handwritten notes.

Richard McKeown

We should not expect
to be forgiven of more than
we are willing to forgive others.

Leave The Last Cookie For Someone Else

The people on the TV screen
should not be more important
than the person across the room.

Richard McKeown

The world is meant to be seen
through a window, not in a mirror.

Leave The Last Cookie For Someone Else

We discipline those we love.
We punish those we're mad at.

Richard McKeown

Quantity of words
does not necessarily reflect
quality of thought.

Leave The Last Cookie For Someone Else

Knowing the right questions
can be better than
having all the answers.

Richard McKeown

Amending our ways
does not mean
abandoning our principles.

Leave The Last Cookie For Someone Else

One of the best ways to
bond with small children is
to get on the floor with them.

Richard McKeown

Not meaning to
is not the same as
meaning not to.

Leave The Last Cookie For Someone Else

The one who says
"I'll forgive, but I'll never forget!"
does neither.

Richard McKeown

A small home is better than a big house.

Leave The Last Cookie For Someone Else

Strive to be educated,
not merely validated.

Richard McKeown

Lawns are sprayed on.
Yards are played on.

Leave The Last Cookie For Someone Else

Mavericks don't make good teammates.

Richard McKeown

Live as you want
to be remembered.

Leave The Last Cookie For Someone Else

Most people have a hand
in creating most of their problems.

Richard McKeown

The young are courageous
because they don't know what it costs.

The old are courageous
because they don't care what it costs.

Leave The Last Cookie For Someone Else

The question isn't usually
"what's the right thing to do?"

It's "will we choose to do the right thing?"

Richard McKeown

The notion we can do anything
we set our minds to is not true.

Everyone can do some things;
maybe even a lot of things.

But we cannot do everything.
Nor should we try.

Leave The Last Cookie For Someone Else

Tolerance is neither vice nor virtue
until coupled with
what is being tolerated.

Richard McKeown

Quick and easy recipes
are usually not the best recipes.

Leave The Last Cookie For Someone Else

The best way to thank
and honor our mentors
is to become a mentor.

Richard McKeown

What we would never say
or want to be seen doing in our homes
should not be heard
or watched in our homes.

Leave The Last Cookie For Someone Else

Always take the high road.
It's always less crowded.

Richard McKeown

The most gratifying praise
that parents receive
comes from others
about their children.

Leave The Last Cookie For Someone Else

Truth is truth no matter who believes it.
A lie is a lie no matter who believes it.

Richard McKeown

Reacting
should not be confused
with responding.

Leave The Last Cookie For Someone Else

Playing it safe can be risky.

Richard McKeown

Those estranged from
more than one family member
are probably responsible.

Leave The Last Cookie For Someone Else

Learn as much as you can
about as much as you can.

Richard McKeown

Truth is to be declared, not defined.

Leave The Last Cookie For Someone Else

To assert there are no absolutes
is to assert there are.

Richard McKeown

Like birds, good parents
prepare their young
to thrive outside the nest.

Leave The Last Cookie For Someone Else

No matter how much you love money,
it will never love you back.

Richard McKeown

You will always remember
the names of your teammates.

Leave The Last Cookie For Someone Else

Integrity is doing
what we know we should do,
whether we want to or not.

Richard McKeown

The people at the gym are looking
at themselves, not at you.

Leave The Last Cookie For Someone Else

The expectation of success
makes it a probability.

The expectation of failure
makes it a certainty.

Richard McKeown

Each day should include thirty minutes
of solitude, stillness and silence.

Leave The Last Cookie For Someone Else

Volunteer for something.

Richard McKeown

It's okay to look your age.
It's even better to act it.

Leave The Last Cookie For Someone Else

It's easy to find fault in others
when we refuse to see it in ourselves.

Richard McKeown

Children remember and treasure
the time spent with them
more than the money spent on them.

Leave The Last Cookie For Someone Else

The best way to add hours to
the day is to turn off the television.

Richard McKeown

Making threats is usually pointless.

Leave The Last Cookie For Someone Else

No one can offend you
without your permission.

Richard McKeown

Shouting impairs hearing.

Leave The Last Cookie For Someone Else

When in doubt, don't.

Richard McKeown

When wondering if you should say something, ask yourself: "What good will it do?"

Leave The Last Cookie For Someone Else

Read.

Richard McKeown

The risk of action in a matter
should be weighed against
the risk of inaction in the matter.

Leave The Last Cookie For Someone Else

A challenge is not necessarily an attack.

Richard McKeown

Know why you believe
what you believe.

Leave The Last Cookie For Someone Else

The adult described
as 'just a big ole kid' is usually
immature and irresponsible.

Richard McKeown

Successful people do what others won't
and don't do what others will.

Leave The Last Cookie For Someone Else

Anyone raising children
should bear in mind
boys are like dogs
and girls are like cats.

Richard McKeown

The skeptic wonders
if a thing should be done.

The cynic declares it can't.

Leave The Last Cookie For Someone Else

History did not begin
on the day we were born.

Richard McKeown

When others lie about you
and betray you,
get over it and move on.

It's a pretty sure bet they have.

Leave The Last Cookie For Someone Else

Those making a comfortable living
playing something, like a game,
a role or an instrument,
have a pretty good thing going.

Richard McKeown

Living by exceptions is no way to live.

Leave The Last Cookie For Someone Else

Ethics are to be foundational,
not situational.

Richard McKeown

Those never content with all they have
will never be content with all they want.

Leave The Last Cookie For Someone Else

When having to choose
between form or function,
go with function.

Richard McKeown

If you're sorry about something,
just say so and leave it at that.
With no ifs, ands or buts.

Leave The Last Cookie For Someone Else

We are composites of the people,
places and situations
with which we surround ourselves.

Richard McKeown

If you won't say it to someone's face,
don't say it to anyone.

Leave The Last Cookie For Someone Else

If your explanation takes longer
than their accusation,
they probably have a point.

Richard McKeown

There is a profound difference between a happy circumstance and a contented life.

Leave The Last Cookie For Someone Else

Never confuse merit with grace.

Richard McKeown

Some are motivated
by a pat on the back,
others by a kick
in the seat of the pants.

Wise are the parents, coaches
and leaders who know this.

Leave The Last Cookie For Someone Else

Opinions are one thing.
Informed opinions are another.

Richard McKeown

Those who complain the most contribute the least.

Leave The Last Cookie For Someone Else

Listening to someone's problems
can be more helpful
than trying to solve their problems.

Richard McKeown

Gossip spreads when watered,
not when planted.

Leave The Last Cookie For Someone Else

Make decisions based
on what you know,
not on what you wish.

Richard McKeown

**Self-pity is difficult
when serving others.**

Leave The Last Cookie For Someone Else

Regretting what we didn't do
can be more regrettable
than what we did do.

Richard McKeown

Calories we don't consume
are calories we don't have to burn.

Leave The Last Cookie For Someone Else

Influence outlives power.

Richard McKeown

Blessings, no matter how many,
tend to be taken for granted.

Adversities, no matter how few,
tend to be resented.

Leave The Last Cookie For Someone Else

Credit isn't deserved
for doing the right thing
only after it becomes
the expedient thing.

Richard McKeown

Every temptation is a test of integrity.

Leave The Last Cookie For Someone Else

Children want to
be proud of their parents too.

Richard McKeown

It's possible to discuss and disagree
without being disgusting
and disagreeable.

Leave The Last Cookie For Someone Else

Those who talk to you about others
will talk to others about you.

Richard McKeown

**The best toys for children
don't have to be turned on or off.**

Leave The Last Cookie For Someone Else

Anyone thinking about retiring should first watch daytime television eight hours a day for an entire week.

Richard McKeown

Anger is like a lighted match.
It burns those who hold on to it.

Leave The Last Cookie For Someone Else

Adversity fosters tenacity,
if we let it.

Affluence fosters complacency,
if we let it.

Richard McKeown

Never confuse motion with progress.

Leave The Last Cookie For Someone Else

Wishing for everything without doing anything accomplishes nothing.

Richard McKeown

Principles apply to all people
in all situations all of the time.

They become preferences when
applied to some people in some
situations some of the time.

They become meaningless
when not applied to ourselves.

Leave The Last Cookie For Someone Else

It's really hard to sneeze
with our eyes open.

It's just as hard to learn
with our mouths open.

Richard McKeown

Sometimes it's best
to just walk away.

Leave The Last Cookie For Someone Else

Don't be quick to believe the negative, especially when it's about people.

Richard McKeown

Call your parents while you can.

Leave The Last Cookie For Someone Else

The life of the party isn't someone
you want to spend
the rest of your life with.

Richard McKeown

Rarely is anything as bad as it seems
at three o'clock in the morning.

Leave The Last Cookie For Someone Else

If you want everyone
to know something,
tell someone not to
tell it to anyone.

Richard McKeown

People criticize others the most
for that which lies hidden
within themselves.

Leave The Last Cookie For Someone Else

Every now and again,
take the back roads.

Richard McKeown

Children longer remember
who was at their game
than who won their game.

Leave The Last Cookie For Someone Else

There's usually a difference
between someone's
last offer and their final offer.

Richard McKeown

Rarely must we have today what we didn't even know existed yesterday.

Leave The Last Cookie For Someone Else

When someone demands a
yes or no decision 'right now,'
it's best to say no.

Richard McKeown

Be suspicious of those
who are the hero or victim
in all their stories.

Be suspicious of their stories, too.

Leave The Last Cookie For Someone Else

Old friends can't be made
out of new ones.

Richard McKeown

Accidents involve chance.
Mistakes involve choice.

Leave The Last Cookie For Someone Else

It's good to be your children's friend
when they become adults.

In the meantime,
it's better to be their parent.

Richard McKeown

Teachers who students call the toughest
are teachers graduates call the best.

Leave The Last Cookie For Someone Else

The gifts people make for you
are the ones you'll keep.

Richard McKeown

Those who seek credit
rarely deserve it.

Leave The Last Cookie For Someone Else

Putting a price on something
declares its value.

Richard McKeown

When tempted to complain
about a young server in a restaurant,
remember they are someone's child.'

Leave The Last Cookie For Someone Else

Rarely are meetings
more important than recitals.

Richard McKeown

If you have to find something
to spend your money on,
give it to someone who needs it.

Leave The Last Cookie For Someone Else

Contentment is when
all you have is all you want.

Richard McKeown

The beach is a great social equalizer.

Leave The Last Cookie For Someone Else

When a child refers to you as
'Mr.' or 'Mrs.' or 'Sir' or 'Ma'am',
don't insist they stop.

Richard McKeown

No one's life is better
because alcohol is in it.

Leave The Last Cookie For Someone Else

The short-sighted ask
'What will it require?'

The far-sighted ask
'What will it return?'

Richard McKeown

People remember
people who remember
their birthdays.

Leave The Last Cookie For Someone Else

Some of life's fondest memories
involve family dinner
around the kitchen table.

Richard McKeown

Fathers should assure their daughters
it's okay to say, "I can't" right up
to the moment they say "I do."

Leave The Last Cookie For Someone Else

Achievement comes
when we start doing some things
and stop doing others.

Richard McKeown

If life was fair,
we wouldn't have what we have.

Leave The Last Cookie For Someone Else

It's good to develop a skill involving doing something with our hands.

Richard McKeown

Politics shouldn't
destroy friendships.

Leave The Last Cookie For Someone Else

Tradition is not inherently bad
and innovation inherently good.

Neither is tradition inherently good
and innovation inherently bad.

Richard McKeown

If it's true youth is
wasted on the young,
it's also true wisdom is
wasted on the old.

Leave The Last Cookie For Someone Else

Courage can be costly.
So can compliance.

Richard McKeown

As much can be learned
from those who disagree with us
as from those who don't.

Leave The Last Cookie For Someone Else

Just because we can
doesn't mean we should.

Richard McKeown

The more the entitled
expect to come to them,
the less others expect
to come from them.

Leave The Last Cookie For Someone Else

Why not you?

Richard McKeown

It's good to keep moving as much
as we can for as long as we can.

Leave The Last Cookie For Someone Else

Giving advice is easier than taking it.

Richard McKeown

The longer we live,
more and more
matters less and less.

But what does matter,
matters more and more.

Leave The Last Cookie For Someone Else

Who and what we will want
near and dear on our last day
should be who and what
we hold near and dear today.

Richard McKeown

Live a life that will be worth missing.

Leave The Last Cookie For Someone Else

Philippians 3:12-14

Richard McKeown

Leave The Last Cookie For Someone Else

For information regarding
seminars & speaking engagements,
contact:

Richard McKeown
richard@richardmckeown.com
http://www.linkedin.com/in/richardmckeown
www.richardmckeown.com

Made in the USA
Coppell, TX
09 December 2021